T0193222

VISION
of the
LIGHT

A JOURNEY TO GLORY

Katherine Archibold

WESTBOW
P R E S S®
A DIVISION OF THOMAS NELSON
& ZONDERVAN

WestBow Press books may be ordered through booksellers or by contacting:

WestBow Press
A Division of Thomas Nelson & Zondervan
1663 Liberty Drive
Bloomington, IN 47403
www.westbowpress.com
844-714-3454

ISBN: 978-1-6642-9773-9 (sc)
ISBN: 978-1-6642-9772-2 (e)

Library of Congress Control Number: 2023906999

Print information available on the last page.

WestBow Press rev. date: 06/20/2023

A special thanks to God, for his holy inspiration.
To my mother for her endless exhortation and prayers.
To my husband for his wonderful support and the six
pieces in this collection he transformed into song.
To Zoe Myers for her unconditional support in the editing process.
To many others who have shown their love to me on my journey.

Contents

A Letter to the Risen Church

I bring news to you, to all of the nations, and to a global community of fellow believers. I bring a message to all the pastors of the saints, the missionaries of the faith, the laypersons of the denominations, the apostolic ministries, and all those who seek hope.

My life purpose is to deliver this message and lead you into the consecration of it. The Christian Church has done well since the times of early Christendom. It has persevered ruthlessly through the test of time, preserved itself as the salt of the earth and the light of the hill, the hope of the lost, and has been the comfort of the ill and heavy laden. The Word of God has been preached, taught, and delivered to every corner of the earth regardless of the trials of believers and has been the resistance to the evils of men.

Amongst the division of the church, God is now calling for a unified consortium on the understanding and delivery of worship during the end times as a preparatory period for the marriage and consecration of God's people to the Holy Lamb. The Bride and the Groom, the Church and Christ, respectively, are soon to wed, and the wedding arrangements must be initiated. Worship today is not being sufficiently pleasing to the Lord as it must be, and I pray that this letter and narrative collection of poetic prose may shed wisdom on the Lord's true desire.

This is a request for the Church to begin seeking the essence of God's glory, through sanctification and worship. This is the Lord's will upon us, His people. He seeks true worshippers, in spirit and in truth, to worship Him. (John 4:23)

What is *in truth*? It is a Gospel-believing, Trinity-inspired, Christ-centered, Bible-based, doctrine-liberated truth — that salvation through the Lord's grace and the law of justification shall set you free. The conviction of the new birth of the Holy Spirit in you, through the means of baptism, will guide and instruct you into wholeness and sanctification. As one church, our responsibility is to preserve the truth above all, as the treasure inside the lantern that must be carried through the journey of tribulation and must remain intact as the King's wedding gift. The coming end times will shake and thunder misery and ails, and the cries of God's people will bring forth the sound of the trumpets.

What is *in spirit*? It is the full surrender of ourselves to God, making less of our nature in the flesh to give space to the filling of the Holy Spirit in us. May it be that through this experience, our entire being (hearts and minds) be transformed as we fully immerse ourselves in His divine presence and manifestation.

Glorified worship here on earth is the prelude to eternal worship in the Kingdom of God forevermore. It is a passionate, energy-filled, sweat-drenching, heart-poured-out glimpse of experiencing God — like it will be on the day we meet Him, the day we have yearned to see Him, wed Him, lay with Him. It is God's Spirit in us, manifested inside of us, becoming one with us. It is Spirit-filled. Spirit-driven. Spirit-led. Spirit-manifested worship and truth.

We are not butterfly princesses that must ask and request demands upon our King. We are to marry the King of all times and the Ruler of all lands and we must in excellence motivate his deepest desires. We must be ready and sanctified. There will be no inhibitions, no excuses, no regrets on the excellent wedding day. That day will be of the greatest glory and splendor —greater than that of the day of Pentecost or even any glimpse of glory humankind could or ever will experience.

As one Church, we must together prepare the Bride to meet her Groom. God is yearning for a people that are pure in heart. He wants a heart-pour out of His people – a revival that awakens the apathy of our generations. He wants an awakening of those that live in true conviction as born-again believers. People who hunger and thirst for righteousness and continually seek God's everlasting grace – a people that crave to experience God in an unquenching, insatiable way. Our motivations should not be to just crave the blessings and promises of prosperity from God. Ultimately, instead, He wants to bless His true servants, those so meek, so poor in spirit, who yearn earnestly to see His Face.

God designed worship as an act of pleasure and wonder as a profound mystery of the intimacy and presence of the light of God. It is not just about kinetic movement, exalted synergy, and exalted pleasure in the climax — it is the ultimate act of love, as illustrated in the Song of Solomon. Our 120-year lifespan is merely a preparatory period for the entrance to the Kingdom. As the feminine role player, we are to prepare our hearts, our passion, and our stamina for the glorious day. The Groom is already prepared as the groom is always so eager in expectation, but the Bride is the one that has to give herself over in consecration. We must be ready to give all of ourselves. We must submit to the beautifying and purifying rituals of wedding ceremonies. Do not let yourselves be stained or tarnished during this time. We must come as one, not as many, as a complete union in spirit and truth. We must let go of all divisiveness, selfishness, all vanity. Servitude shall not be intended to bring attention to ourselves, but, in our devotion, grounded on a sacrificial love that gives all glory to God.

The encounter is at the wedding reception. The opening act will be our first real encounter with God. We will profoundly know God. We will seal the covenant. It is a prelude with an opening scene and many sequels to come. We must prepare for our presentation to be worthy of the King of Kings. The grand orchestra will have many sectionals. The prophets, pastors, evangelists, singers, worshippers, prayer warriors, and all those with spiritual gifts will come together to lead the grand festive.

Glorified worship is God's ultimate burnt offering. Glorified worship is not to be static; it is not to be motionless. It is not just about music or a sermon. It is a caliber of movements and precision of adoration of praise and seduction. It is above all pure and aesthetically pleasing to the Lord. It is not a choreographed dance. It is not a setup of cameras, stage, dress, or props. It is not a performance. In its glorified form, worship is not singers and instrumentalists on stage, it is true worship on the altar. It is not filled with emotion; it is filled with experiencing the manifestation of the Holy Ghost. It is not egocentric. It is not glory-seeking. It has no void. It has all meaning. It is a story to tell of devotion, sacrifice, thanksgiving, praise, confession, supplication, and immersion. As we dive into the wellsprings of abundant love, joy, and peace in God, our Lord, we reconcile ourselves to His will and purpose for our existence.

This message has been delivered to me by a series of dreams and visions. I have been blessed to see the purpose of our existence – the glory and splendor we were eternally birthed for.

At the wedding reception, there will be hundreds dancing and singing in adoration and praise along with ancient and modern instruments, clothed in white, the masses will move to the sounds of the glory of the heavens. It is to be a magnificent heavenly celebration of ancient Jewish

Hasidic-style dances such as Horah and Yemenite steps. Reunited families rejoicing together. Joy, fulfillment, and wholly devotion will overpower the dances and postures. The great spokespersons and musicians leading will be just sections in the heavens but the masses will be the altar. Sections of the masses will give flow to the waves of the oceans of worshippers, and individual expression will be the way to adoration and exaltation. Oh, how I yearn to experience all this with all my fellow believers.

We are the risen church. We are the hope of this time, the remnant of the days of Elijah, Joshua's generation. We get the opportunity to experience a taste of glorified worship now. Let us do our preparations well. Let us serve God with the proper heart and intention. Together, we as the Bride will wed soon and see glory outpour from the wellsprings of creation. We will wed the great Alpha and Omega, and with Him, our Creator, we will birth a new beginning – a new time when we will enjoy God's goodness in the absence of all suffering. Together we will worship the Lord for eternity and bask in His everlasting glory.

His Echo in Us

don't you know who He is?
the Enigma of Life,
the ghost of time, the limits of space divine.
do you know the makeup behind His mask?
can you even begin to fathom His glory alive?

in the void of the dark,
He is the form that gives light.
He is the Father of all, the Maker of the depths and the waves.
He is the Voice of the Ages, relentless, infinite,
Creator of all that is and all to be.

He is the Grand Clockmaker, the Keeper of Time,
the Great Architect of the natural laws,
the Pure Source of the endless dawns,
and the Master Composer of the mysteries of the stars.
His Spirit is life, His Word, alive.

His breath, His synergy, materialized
the dust trail of the cosmos,
His intention, His logic crystallized
whose remnant resonates, vibrates, radiates.
His echo is the resemblance of His essence.

hear the power of His mighty gears!
His Spirit is the locomotor of volition;
volition engrossed in power, that echoes motion;
motion, the reaction of a chemical explosion.
divine is the echo that births forth His presence,
mighty, radiant, transcendent.

stark is the mark of His zeal
that grasps the redemption of humankind.
His seed, a.k.a. His own form of offspring
is His breath made alive,
mass made into life, His Word formed into flesh,
the conception of His essence, His glory divine.

the material essence of the Great Echo of time;
the vast, great space of the Great Echo contained;
the Echo of Alpha, the beginning of all that is;
the Echo of Omega, the end of all forever will be;
His presence with us, His Echo in us.

The Glory of Creation

You are He who is the Great I Am!
He who under the sun emits and encompasses all the cosmos,
the one whose essence radiates everlasting.
He who is the Alpha and the Omega,
the one who beholds all the stars and the elements!
He who is the Creator of all the dimensions,
the one designer of the tree of life.
He who is Zion, the Lion of Judah,
the one Maker of rain, air, and light!

You are He who is the Usher of Promise,
the Master of the waters, winds, and fire!
He who is the Bearer of the Great Essence,
the presence that preludes the great enigma.
He is the substance of the equilibrium of the forces,
who balances the electromagnetic orbits.
He who is the Meridians of the Compass of Life,
the firmament of the holy glory.
He who holds the key to the souls of humankind,
the sole governor by the authority of order and love!

You are He who is the doer by messianic birth!
You are He who is the heir by divine order!
You are He who is the dignitary of the rite of life!
He who is the ruler of the angels of the universe!

He who is the guardian of the affairs of the sacred,
of those blessed inheritors of the prize of the beatitudes!
He who evolves by the zeal of honor and praise,
emerging from Your secret dwelling
to preside over the sacred temple!

allow us, who desire the essence of both
Your reproach and pleasure,
to be reassured by Your mightiness.
let us know Your light, joy, and peace
for our eyes of flesh cannot fathom the Great Glory,
a mirror greater than
the splendor of the skies and heavens!

oh Yahweh
in whom we trust!

You are He who will defeat the pigs of Helena —
those who call upon two faiths under the sun
You angsted against Elif, the Doer of War
the Wolf foe of Enir, Elif the Droll.
for then clothed like the angel of the light, the Alavinth of Elif,
purebred of both the Cobra and the Wolverine,
ate of both the bosom of the tree of knowledge and the bosom of the
tree of life

the Alavinth of Elif, the great archenemy of the peace of the nations,
declared the foe of Tejar, foe of Hira the Droll;
brother by birth, doer by order of Baalah;
wary of the birthright of Elif
and rose when Troy worshiped and was loved
by the New York of the Old York. **

You are the Supreme Judge, the Chief Restorer.
You are the One Litigator of the impunity of the evils of humankind,
of the sin of our wretchedness.
the one who calls judgment to the begotten—
those who wandered away in the Wilderness of Double Edge,
those who lay aimless and withered in ignorance's fate,
those who succumbed to the passivity of the ages.

pour out the anointing on your army,
the diligent biota of the fields.
search us truly, oh great Hosanna!
search the deepest dimensions of our beings.
find in us the essence of a pure heart,
and bless us with the presence of Your Sublime Essence
let us serve You now; let us boldly call up a great consensus.
though glory is the unspoken harvest,
the blessed fruits of the Spirit,
let our hearts rejoice in You,
singing the wonderful song of bountiful life!

God Is Life

Faith is what ignites us
the energy, the essence of Life
God is the balance
the orbit, of day and night
Faith, is the source of exertion
ignition, prowess, and passion
motion, conviction, and compassion
God is our light and fire
Jesus, the water that cleanses us
the Spirit, the wind and air that consumes us
God is Life

A Story of Joys and Sorrows

Part I

the richness of humankind,
the vaulted memories,
the beauty of the canvas of life,
the story to be, human in existence,
to reminisce over the preeminence.

to dance the ballad of life,
to experience the great diversity,
the flavors, the places, the peoples,
the encaustic masterpiece
of the ancient intertwined with the new
that hangs as showpieces in the great halls,
the galleries, the timeless work of the ages.

this calls for a toast!
to the nostalgia of the days of youth,
the liveliness of things anew,
to the pleasures of the smiles,
the voices, the expressions, the touches,
the touch of grace, a glimpse of favor,
the motions that vibrate, the chimes, and the strings,
the rings that cry victory!

to a story that begins
with the sounds of laughter,
to the warmth of sitting by company,
the humor, the rich pleasures, the laughs,
the proximity of strangers, the joys of guests,
the smokes of cigars, the vibrant colors, the textures,
the shuffles of the malls and city markets,
the tastes of the palettes, the grand dinner parties,
the clubs, and the bars,
the lounges, the cafés, the ball games,
the roar of the fans,
the ambiance of the multitudes in concert.
to the huddle of the sweat, the smells of the breaths,
the fragrances of the rich,
of the littles, of the bigs, of the meek, of the grand.

surely to a life that runs on the drugs of adrenaline and ecstasy
and is then drawn to a halt by a new dawn

Part II

the plague of bane
in the aftermath of the festive the next day
overshadows a worry,
the subtle slogan of dual proponents—
silence bores.

consequently, in contemplation, Life asks,
"if to live is to die, then why do we live?
are we just mounds of flesh, matter to rot?

is that it? is it just the reality that binds us,
only the constraints that limit us,
bind us by the limitations in which we exist?"

Silence begs us to know the reason
of loss, despair,
of pain, and void.
why be born to suffer, to bear life alone,
sunken, soul repressed?

Silence bears the weight.

a plague that is, that refuses to cease,
relentless to be
the great sorrow of humankind,
the hidden slums of the dark places of the bouts of our souls,
the certitude that life will soon be no more.

a pig to be slaughtered, impending doom,
born, to be weaned, to be flattened up,
and then devoured.

Life sings a lament
to the greatest scarcity of all time
to a lack of purpose to be
the greatest need fellow people could know,
the great, looming reality,
the certitude of the face of pure dismay, of disarray.

Part III

the archives of my ancestors' harvest were ransacked.
the bounty, called Truth, was robbed and burned away to dust.
the young are now the bearers of a great drought,
the consequence of the schools of free thought.

the nineteenth century, who vanished God, said,
"Man, you are free—
free to carve out your own masterpiece
with no need to commit
except to indulge in one's self
with no need to give an account of your deeds."

the twentieth century then reasoned and said,
"by simple logic I say,
'Man, since your life counts only to you,
then your existence serves nothing.
if you have no account of your life to give,
then why would your life matter?'"

then the twenty-first century rhetorically reasons,
"am I then no better than a simulation,
a play, a game, just a dream within a dream?
what is it like to be a character in the great rat race?
to run into the endless horizon with no destination,
with no place to mirage the end?"

then the Wind proclaims,
"the windmill has halted.
it's all too mundane.
it is merely all bane and vain."

oh, the sorrow of a caged bird!
cries at the face of the bane, the maze of the vain.
contemplate this: if life has no reason to be, no purpose to persist,
do you know the reason to exist, to be?

oh, woe to the pleasures of the old, the dread of the new.
really? is there anything at all?
something for us to reap, to bestow, a purpose to sow?
is this it? is this all? is this all there is to know?
to live by the truth that only tomorrow knows—
tomorrow, the keeper to the hidden key
that holds the secrets of those who no longer mourn.

Part IV

a reckless train, the engine of the great fret,
the strain of the huddle, of the great hustle
Futility reigns, and at the speed of fury,
the locomotion of the pits resonates.
the echo of foreign caves vibrates.
the climaxes rise, excerpts linger.
the intense exertion pushes, pushes further,
further, and further, just out a little further.

Friend, I ask you,
what is motion with no intention?
if God is the power that ignites, that propels all that is?

oh, woe to you! woe to you who knows Him not!
to be a headless chicken running in circles
membranes fried, saturated, pressed
dejected, wearily suppressed
to know the fear of the uncertain
to think that this life is it
an unrelenting reality in which I refuse to live
why then exist?

no, no, no
I exist to resist, I exist to believe
to be the resistance
a fighter in the war of the biotas of truth
able to adapt, adverse to folly
to be true to that which truly is
rising from the deep, rising to the peak

I know the value of my life to be a miracle,
a form that sustains and continues to be preserved
life of an essence that refuses to decompose
that instead angsts to find the immortal fountain of youth
that brings back the resonance of the glorious choirs
of the great victors of faith, heroes in rescue after the free fall

a life that brings back meaning
and summons the loss of the counts of the days
that were given away to futile waste

Part V

in the way, at the joy of purpose
a clever bird, an innate spirit unrelentingly endures
to survive and thrive
this little songbird that competes to be heard
is one of the mightiest pillars that resonate
pillars that resist the test of time
the test of the elements
pillars that prove their victory
and why they continue to stand

the clever bird declares
"an unpleasant visitor called Void invaded our lands!
woe to you!
bring your burdens home
bring your troubled heart to a place of peace
bring your flowers home to Him!"

in the stillness of time that does not fade
sings a gentle tune that plays dynamo
that calls for hope, summons a ray of hope
then the unfathomable happens…

the clever bird sings
"the Silver Lining of Dawn cometh! we pray for the rain!"
it shouts boldly
"power up the pump! revere the Master!
propagate the seeds of great fertile things to be!
search for the water! seek the light!
lay here at the feet of the fountain of youth!
harness the wind! know the secret of how mysteries flow!"

the little songbird then spins the wheels of time
and sets forth a new motion and tells us to look out the window
eager to see, earnest to hear, the voice of truth
to see our tribes, worship the Lord, our King
to see our sons and daughters bearing the fruits
heirs of our labors of the days old and the days anew

Joy is the lark's song
a free bird indeed
that migrates toward the Great Destination
the presence of the King of Kings
sings a new song, a new melody
the greatest rhapsody of the ages
of love for God, His eyes of fire
a console of a gentle embrace
of love for life, the Kingdom's delight
the spectrum of colors shines forth Wisdom
bearing His Knowledge, His Logic
full of grace and love for people
for all the members that run the same race to the end
to the ends of the age

eager to turn the page, forth to the throne of exaltation
ready to know, eager to bask
yearning to know the greatness of God
to partake in an earthly glimpse of the glory divine
to transcend high on high, to the eternal Kingdom of God
a kingdom that minds cannot begin to fathom
before the reflection of the doors of His heart
at the feet of His greatness

Part VI

shhh, hear where the echo originates
hear a whisper resonating from the deep, shhh

"look!" cries the lark
"look at the glistening seas of beauty and splendor!

and the waves afar say
"let Faith be it!
the reason to exist, to be the flame
the fuel that propels us
that satisfies us fully
that craves to envision a new dream to be
to be the emission, the fuel of all that exists"

motion with intent! life with a profound purpose

the lark bird that thirsts and hungers for both what is
and what is to be
suddenly, hears a fresh sound
and harmonizes to a new beat, sings a new song
a new song called PURPOSE
that emerges deep within
a purpose to be, the reason to exist
that runs the sprints and the highs
the lows and the peaks
the trills and the pauses
the stanzas and the rests

ignited to flame up hope, light up the trek to the hill
on the path of a journey that doesn't relent
to carry us toward the greatest day
to the greatest miracle to come forth, in fullest glory shone
the best yet to come, a moment in conquest determined
unrelenting to continue to endure the good fight
ready to conquer, to ascend to the High Place
to find the lover of our souls that dwells there
and in due time, suspended in glory
to lay motionless before time and space
as we worship Him to the end, the end of the end

Part VII

Friend, join my quest to live a life worth living
as we reach the highest peak of Mighty Glory
eager to be filled in the presence of He Who Is
we to be what He deems us to be
what He dreams us to be

journey with me to the vast eternal dimensions of the unknown
to know sovereign mercy, to treasure the grand falls
to dive in the springs of pure grace, to know the forthright
to transcend through the rite of what is to be
soon to reveal the radiance of what beholds

basking in the joy of splendor, that knows no woes
until eternity indulges the sounds of delight
that sways in the divine melody of the unknown
that floats in the silence, in the purity of His light

that trembles afloat
still, motionless before God Himself

go in the waves of truth, conquer the tide
live in the glory that arises alive
exist to be, in the name of He Who Is, He Who Lives

Time Is To Be

time is to be, to be silent
silent in the stillness
to be still
to hear the vibrations of the utters of silence
to be aware of the chords and the measures of God Divine

to float aboard the great timeline
the pathway to the radiance of eternal life
to exist and to travel the eternal chords of glory
Glory that bears light in the wilderness of day and night
night and day, today and tonight, tonight and today

to travel in warps
through the ages
through the vastness
towards the pureness of Glory Divine
eager to seek, willing to see

to be on the journey to the Great Light
to climb up the highest peak, up the heavenly stairwell
through the passage of the last rite
to transcend the dimensions of what is
what is to be, to earnestly know Who He Is

to know that all that beholds
is to be still before God, in the presence of Glory Alive
at the greatest splendor that radiates ever so brightly
surreally, divinely

Your Perfect Way in Me

have your perfect way in me
make yourself in me complete
in your fullness, I rejoice
at your feet, I find my place
the splendor of your glory is my beat
in your likeness, I go forth
may Your will shine through me

Abide in My Light

In the stillness of a dark night, the Lord whispered softly into my soul, "As you rest in me my child, hear me now. Does not starlight become more pronounced in the backdrop of vast darkness? Do you not know that the darker the wilderness, the brighter the light of my glory? As you have trekked forth in this great journey the bitter cold and endless fatigue have consumed you — may your heart now rest in me."

"Do you not know, my child, your heart, is the *hearth* of my home, the *morada****, meaning the center place of the warmth of this dwelling? For as my Spirit resides in you, in the *hearth* of this dwelling tent, I give you sweet warmth and a divine gentle, loving embrace. By the great mystery of the ages, I desire to make you my own holy dwelling place."

"I am the pillar of fire within you that ceases not to be quenched. Grieve me not, seek always my Glory. Thirst for me, and you will see my Glory, know of my Glory, bask in my Splendor, here in this life and eternally."

"Relinquish yourself to me for I am always to sustain you, provide for you, and protect you. Worry not, for I am always to guide you, instruct you, and show you the way to the truth. I am your light in the midst of the night, and the cool breeze in the heat of the day."

"abide in Me and I will abide in you
be in Me and I will be in you
seek Me and you will find Me
dwell in Me and I will dwell in you
be assured in Me and I will reassure you

know Me and I will know you
surrender to Me and I will free you
lay your burdens unto me and I will bear all the weight for you
stand in Me and I will stand by you

walk in Me and I will walk for you
equip yourself in Me and I will persevere for you
honor Me and I will honor you
be still in Me and I will use you for My Glory"

"For if you preside in my kingdom and let me reign in your heart, you will be as the bird in the sky and the lily in the fields. Bask now in my Light and I will be the splendor that shines in you, around you, and through you. May my Spirit forever, now and eternally, abide in your heart, my beloved child."

As the Lord's divine words struck the depths of my soul and He concluded his message to me, His peace overwhelmed me. As I closed my eyes, I began to drift into a profound sleep. I rested fully assured, knowingly and certain that as I would continue my journey at daybreak, He was with me. Then, in a soft vibration of wonder, 2 Corinthians 3:18 echoed in my heart… I, with an unveiled face, beholding as in a mirror the glory of the Lord, am being transformed into the same image from glory to glory, by the Spirit of the Lord.

You Turn My Mourning Into Dancing

there is a pain that aches
a pain that screams, o woe to me

as the end of the journey lingers on
as the darkness warps the void
O, Great Reedemer of my soul, hear my cry

come for me in the pits of these eerie valleys
carry me and heal my deepest wounds
open the floodgates of heaven
have your armies deliver to me your mercies
for I know the battle may be lost
but the war my God has won

for the pain my soul partakes cannot destroy me
for the despair cannot choke me
for when your power saturates me
in You, I am fearless, avidly relentless

allow me to partake of the divine nature
trade in sorrow for the joy of your glory
dead in my flesh, I call upon the strength of your bosom
I am encouraged by the testament of your sovereignty

Your Spirit lives in me, I am alive
for I am Yours and You are mine

Your victory will overcome the raging floods
Your power will restore the wastelands lost
You will redeem the fruit the wildfires consumed
give way to me renewed, to life anew

in stillness
I listen to the mysteries Hosanna whispers
I will follow the Choirmaster's voice out from this wilderness
crescendo to the peaks of brilliance
transfigure past the climax of everlasting radiance
dancing in the winds that blow me to eternal bliss

You give new dawn in me
You turn my mourning into dancing
the trumpets blasting give life to these dry bones
I dance to the rhythm of jubilee
Victory Magnificent!

hear my new song from the passion that stirs within me
hear me say in You I am invincible
that no stronghold can defeat me
that no enemy can stand against me
O merciful Savior
hear me sing that victory is Yours forever
You reign on Your throne that glows radiantly
eternally, splendidly

A Psalm of Love

Part I

indeed, my senses may be exemplary
colors are bright, taste buds dance
olfactories retract, tympanies resonate, epidermis senses touch
but through my own spectacles, I cannot see

my blindness suggests a discourse
my ignorance then boldly asks five questions

in a mission accomplished as a specimen
one more soul sanctioned by the Spirit
am I one more creation
sentenced to the morbid, which I am destined?

a fetus born to a world of despair
nothing beholds it more than the lunacy of desperation —
am I one more joined to the brotherhood
the brotherhood of doomed mortality
by the looming fire of destruction?

an inferior pawn trapped in a war between supernatural forces
present between the realms of superior foes —
whose power shall prevail
ultimately win one more of me from the multitudes out of the horizon?

why would a father allow one more child
to come into a world possessed by evil?

to then let him dance on the beam between the high places?

Part II

how I yearn to be filled by the Spirit
how I long for these blind eyes of flesh
to see the light of Your Glory
how I long for these deaf ears
to hear of Your Living Proclamation
how I long for these mute lips
to speak of Your Holy Grace and Truth

O my Redeemer, carry my crippled self
into the Holy Place of Your Dwelling
comfort and renew me with Your Divine Love
for Your Divine Love is Your Greatest Promise
as I hunger and thirst to see Your Promises

then, in a cloud of glory, You reveal Yourself
"my child, the holy answer --- is love
to fulfill the grand, sacred story of wondrous love"

Part III

how I long to taste the flavors and delicacies of Your Creation
to smell the sweetness of Your Goodness
how I long to read through the Story of Your Greatness

for my mind to discern Your Wisdom
how I long to decipher Your Revelations
to know You by Thy Holy Trinity

how I long to touch the vapor, chase the wind
to capture the dust of Your Everlasting Power
how I long to understand Your Sovereignty
to know entirely Your Right and Left
how I yearn to be comforted by the blanket of Your Affection
to know of Your Complex Mysteries, Coded Revelations, and Glorious
Wonders

and at the sight of Your Presence, to be deemed worthy
to perceive in clarity only Your Voice
to be touched by Your Gentle Stillness
and to be able to fathom the holy story of Your Magnificence!

Part IV

O, how You love me, my Adonai!
I shall know of Your Tender Mercies
by the Holiness of the Holy
by the Sacrifice of Your Pure Grace and Justification
by Your Promise of Love
You make known Your Divine Timeline!

You are our holy measuring totem called Christ
You are the Messianic gift of our deliverance
You are the finite solution to the perfect algorithm of life

You are Infinite Love, our Lamb
who we are soon to wed and miraculously behold

Your Divinity is the universal design of life
furthermore, even incomparable to Your Eternal Glory
Your Promise of the splendor of the heavens reigns forever!
Your Glory and Love shall prevail forever!

Miracles

I saw the mountains fly
and heard "GLORY!" the chorus cry
and they sang:

I heard the trumpets blast
the walls of Jericho collapse
I saw myself a wretched sinner
from the ashes rise

I heard a mute sing
I saw a fish walk
I saw a turtle sprint
I saw the Red Sea part

I saw the brightest night sky
I saw the heavens open
I saw the brightest light shine
I saw the King welcome me to His feast!

Worship at the Heavenly Court

the King shines in splendor
as the masses worship
the masses worship as roaring,
towering epiphanies in chorus
sectionals sway in gorgeous movement,
in rhythms never heard before
explosive, passionate
is the glorious event
a divine beautiful new song
pauses suspended in glory
sounds heard in the depths
beyond the infinite horizon
instruments in multiple orchestras
create innovative cycles of glorious masterpieces
waves of masses come to halt,
then rush to the climax of the precipice
the oceans of worshippers
reflect the landscapes of clouds of many skies
heavens in glory sing together.
All declare He is holy, holy, holy

Oh hallelujah, hallelujah, hallelujah

Oh holy, holy, holy is Your name
Oh sanctus, sanctus, sanctus Tibi est nomen
Oh santo, santo, santo sea Tu nombre

Oh we worship You, worship You, worship Your holiness
Oh gloria, gloria, gloria in the highest place
Oh glory, glory, glory to Your name

Oh we praise You, praise You, praise Your majesty
Oh hallowed, hallowed, hallowed be Your name
Oh kadosh, kadosh, kadosh
Oh King of Kings, Lord of Hosts
Oh Adonai Tez-va-out

Oh Yahweh, Yahweh, Yahweh
Oh holy, holy, holy are You
Oh sacred, sacred, sacred is Your love

A Prayer of a Warrior Rising

I seek you O Lord in the early mornings
I seek you endlessly for eternal dawns
search me O my Redeemer
for my eyes in this flesh cannot fathom the glory of heaven!

search me O Lord
for you wove my deep being
search me O Lord
that I may hold no reproof at Your tender mercies

look in me
from down at my South Gate to my North Gate
look in me from my East to my West
may I be blameless at Your sight

the corners of my plight bend only to serve You
for it is not a cry of a saint but a broken spirit at war to love
to seek You and to not defile You, my Lord
my King in whom I blindly trust

it is not my righteousness enough
but the bounty of a pure heart
bless me O Lord, my Savior
to fight your Great War
bless me as I dress in Your armor
ready to go out to the battlefield

bless me in such a time as this
that You have prepared me to die to defend the Truth
times of stance and opportunity to serve You
All-Mighty, All-Powerful, All-Consuming God

I cry out my Lord to You!
bless me as I lay with You at this break of dawn
may Your Spirit rest in the subliminal essence of my soul

I send forth a battle cry to the generations
I declare victory to our Lord, the Great I Am
He who sits at the Throne of Everlasting Grace!

I yearn to live in Your presence until I breathe my last sigh
I awake, thanking You for letting me live one more day
and for letting me see another sunrise

please fill my day with joy, love, and peace
shower me with Your Spirit and show me how to walk in faith
dress me grandly in Your mighty armor and help me rise like a warrior
this daybreak!

give me the strength, discipline, and wisdom
to let me bring home the victory this day
give me a sound mind of iron wits
filled with the vitality and vigor I need to conquer this day's giants

take away my deepest pains and fears
take control of the apprehension and uncertainty that life may bring
take away my frustrations and show me the way to righteousness

show me Your way
teach me how to trust in You completely
take my hand as I fully surrender to You this morning
preserve my joy, take me to Your glory!

Your faithful servant,
Your Warrior to Be

Arise! Alive!

death cometh, for I know I am begotten
death hath no grip, for it hath lost its sting on me

bring these dry bones back to life
see these bones in victory arise

I am a warrior that firmly stands
my soul will not relent
my soul will carry on
I will go on declaring what he has done
boldly singing who He is, and what all He made of me

I know You have risen, I rise alike forever alive
I am a victor of Your glory divine
because Your Spirit lives in me, I live

I praise You while I am fallen
I praise You when there is no more breath in me
I praise You in the fierce storms
I praise You on the battlefield
of the war that rages on

sing with me:

O Hosanna of my soul, Glory, Glory, Glory
O Hosanna of our souls, Glory, Glory, Glory

I adore You, O lover of my soul
we adore You, O lover of our souls

arise! rise in the name of Jesus!
arise! rise in the power of His Name!
Mighty, Mighty is Your Name

Frontline

I am the Frontline.
make of me the engineer of the building of our New Dwelling,
the strategist of the Modern Dynamic,
an advocate of You, the Judge of the Great Trial,
I am she, a woman after Your Heart!

I am the remnant bride-to-be of the Old Covenant,
and now the bride of the New Pact awaiting Your Return!
the pact of the promise of our ancestors,
the kings, and the royal priesthood of the testaments

I am the essence of two,
mother-to-be of the rebirth
of the yearnings of the Jews and Gentiles,
chosen by the royal lineage of the Holy Lamb.

by faith and confession, calvary and sacrifice,
I am the resonance of the battle cry of the mighty warriors,
the Battalion of the War of Justice and Glory,
the fighter of the battles of Old, by the kindred of New.
the Old made New,
under the declaration of His Handiwork,
that declared the Great Rescue mission,
armed by the power and grace of the Grand Redemption,
and the holy design of Your Divine Archetype,
the Southeast to the Gates and the Northwest to the Wells.

I am she who will exhort the sons and daughters of our royal priesthood
to rise to the calling,
the calling of the righteous and sanctification of the holy saints,
calling believers back to the craft of faith and reason.

I am she who will express the desires of You, the Holy Trinity,
the reflections of radiance, breath, and vitals
as Your Divine Motive,
exhorting true worshippers to worship in spirit and in truth.

bring forth the wise elders of the Great Sedar,
the fermented harvest,
and the fragrances of the sweetness of Your Joy!

Anthem for Revival

Yahweh, God our Father
You created all, all that is
You made form, you gave life
You are the maker of all that is

Holy Spirit
work Your power
bring down the heavens
be that fire that burns our passion

Yeshua, Messiah
Son of God, and Son of Man
on Your cross,
through Your pain
You made all things
bear fresh new air

I believe the Word of God
the truth in which I abide
I dance the way
sing the truth
see the light
to the Kingdom of God

You take my sins and all I lack
gift me grace
fill my hope with everlasting life

the power of Your blood washed me clean
baptized me for the resurrection
and born again I rise today
by the Spirit of God that lives in me
we are the remnant that rises today together in power this latter-day
we worship as we wait for the Lord's return before the end of days
we rest on the promise of the eternal blessing, of life anew
ready to see the Kingdom of Heaven
we receive the wealth of glory forever
glory, glory, glory, glory
and forever, ever, and ever we praise Your mighty name
the testament of our faith

Amen

Christ's Newness

Inspired By Havdalah[****]

defile the dark
define the light

wake up! there's much work awaiting
wake up! sense the new awakening

it's time for harvest
time to smell the sweet spices
time to smell the wine done fermenting

a new week has begun
arise mighty this dawn
the darkness for too long has had no mercy or tithings
arise now for our Savior's triumph is the Good News shining brightly

the past is waste
but new greatness is awaiting
the past is lost
but fresh is the beginnings birthing forth from mighty holiness
the past is past
but the scent of joy has resurrected, springing forth a glorious morning

Endnotes

** a fictionalized account of the fall of Satan and the one-third of the angels that were cast down from heaven, Satan's deception of Adam and Eve that led to the fall of mankind, and the order and establishment of the pagan gods during the ancient times that led subsequently to the wars of the nations

*** *morada*: house, abode, dwelling, from Spanish *morar* to live, dwell, from Latin *morari* to remain, to be actively present, to devote attention to

****originating from Old Testament times, a Hebrew ceremony or formal prayer ritual that marks the end of the Sabbath or a festival and ushers in a new week celebrated by lighting a special candle, blessing the wine, and smelling sweet spices

About the Author

Meet Katherine Archibold.

She is a writer, artist, and entrepreneur.

She was trained as a prodigy at the Conservatorio de Cali - Escuela Departamental de Bellas Artes and later pursued the tutelage of Angel Rayo, her uncle, influenced by her family heritage of Colombian artist legend, Omar Rayo. In South Florida during her youth, Katherine became a student and instructor apprentice of Conchita Firgau, the great Venezuelan master painter. Katherine's first passion is the visual arts, and oil is her preferred medium.

As a writer, Katherine has produced several collections of poetry, which are under review for publishing, and she enjoys sharing her voice through the poetic medium of spoken word rhetoric. Her art portfolio can be found at _www.zionsprouts.com/art_.

Above all, she is a worshipper with an unending love for praise and worship. Expanding on her previous work that emphasizes our primitive natures and innate survival mechanisms, her ongoing work focuses on shifting the focus from man's inward condition to the magnificent beauty and great complexity of Creation.

Through intellectual rigor and avid pursuits in the arts, she attempts to bridge the gap between science and faith using multi-sensorial mediums in combination with aesthetic, naturalistic, and divine inspirations to create a concise, clear illustration of the everlasting glory of God.

Katherine has successfully transformed her ideas into business ventures throughout the years and her current venture, ZION Sprouts, is a collaborative effort with her husband, Michael Richardson.

About the Composer

Meet Michael D. Richardson.

His voice has been said to "transcend the listener to glory" and to "transform the human spirit to find God". He is a Verdi baritone gifted with a dramatic contrast of a hefty weight of nobility in the color of his sound. Michael's dramatic voice combination, of a big, rich-sounding caliber, ringing high notes, and the stamina to sit extensively in the high range is sure to strike you. Mr. Richardson performs in English, French, Italian, German, and Latin.

Michael D. Richardson is an Iowa-born-and-raised vocalist, soloist, and music scholar. He is a doctoral candidate at James Madison University studying under the tutelage of the renowned Canadian baritone, Grammy-winner Kevin Mcmillan, under whom Michael also completed his Master's. Michael completed his Bachelor's at Buena Vista University under Dr. Merrin Guice-Gill.

Michael was the 1st Place Winner in his category at the 2019 National Association of Teachers of Singing (NATS) Competition and Encouragement Award Recipient in the Metropolitan Opera National Competition Districts 2019.

He performed the role of William Putnam in Jake Hagee's opera If I Were You at the Nightingale Opera Theater in 2022. In James Madison University Opera productions, notable roles are those of Nick Shadow in Igor Stravinsky's Rake's Progress in 2022; Leporello in Mozart's Don Giovanni in 2021; Papageno in Die Zauberflöte in 2020; Mephistopheles in Faust in 2019; and George Benton in Dead Man Walking in 2018. He performed Gianni Schicchi in Gianni Schicchi at Buena Vista University Opera in 2017.

He was a soloist in 2019 in the JMU Wind Symphony's rendition of Porgy & Bess's 'Catfish Row' and in Haydn's Creation. From 2010 to 2018, he was a performer and assistant conductor with the Fort Dodge Harmony Brigade.

In the professional sphere, he has been invited to perform soloist roles at various community concerts and has had over 30 invitations as a guest performer in local churches. He has also performed in over 20 funerals.

Michael has a great affinity for singing, composing, and archiving collections of sacred music, spirituals, gospel, and praise & worship selections. In his spare time, he has enjoyed performing in barbershop quartets, doing voice-overs, performing in his church, and producing music compilations.

To follow Michael's work, visit *www.michaelrichardsonbaritone.com*!

Printed in the United States
by Baker & Taylor Publisher Services